Canterbury Cathedral

Jonathan Keates & Angelo Hornak

SCALA BOOKS

Contents

©1994 Scala Publishers Ltd

First published in 1980 by
Summerfield Press Limited and Philip Wilson Publishers Limited

Revised edition, 1994, 1998
by Scala Publishers Limited
Gloucester Mansions
140a Shaftesbury Avenue, London WC2H 8HD
Text: Jonathan Keates
Photographs: Angelo Hornak
Design: Robin Forster (Art to Go!)
Produced by Scala Publishers Ltd
Printed and bound in Italy

Reprinted in 2002

ISBN 1 85759 027 9 (paperback)

The publishers wish to thank the Dean and Chapter of Canterbury Cathedral for
their encouragement and in particular Canon Peter Brett for his assistance with
many details of the text

The photographer would like to thank the Vesturer and the cathedral staff for their
help and advice

A message from the Dean

Welcome to Canterbury Cathedral. We very much hope that you enjoy this holy and historic place – the seat of the Archbishop of Canterbury as Primate of all England, Diocesan Bishop of the diocese of Canterbury and leader of the Anglican Communion throughout the world. It is both a holy place where worship has been carried on daily for over fourteen hundred years, and part of a World Heritage Site containing many historic treasures. It is also the home of a community made up of many different types of people, all of whom seek to make the Cathedral a place of welcome, beauty and holiness.

There has been a school attached to the Cathedral from the beginning of its life. On the South side of the Precincts is the new International Study Centre, opened in April 2002 to enable Christian leaders, students and other visitors to live and study here as part of the Cathedral community. You will find many things of interest, and this comprehensive guide-book will enhance your knowledge of the Cathedral and Precincts.

Robert Willis.

THE VERY REVEREND ROBERT WILLIS, DEAN OF CANTERBURY

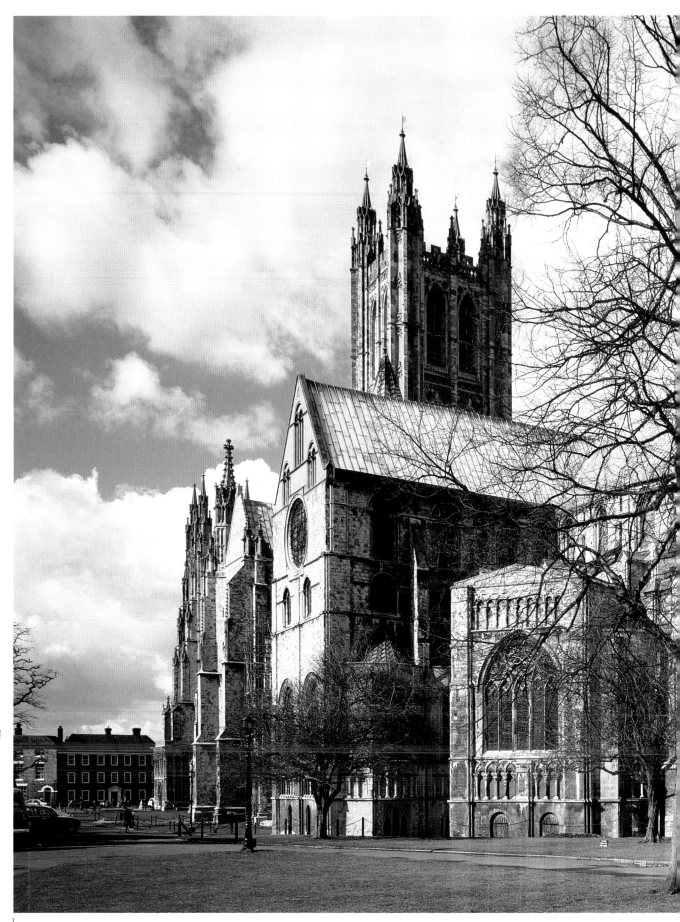

View of the Cathedral from the east.

Chronology to 1900

597	King Ethelbert of Kent baptized by St Augustine
602	The first Cathedral dedicated by St Augustine
668-693	St Theodore, archbishop
960-988	St Dunstan, archbishop
995-1005	Aelfric, archbishop (Benedictine revival)
1006-12	St Alphege, archbishop
1011	Canterbury sacked by the Danes. The Cathedral damaged
1067	The Cathedral destroyed by fire
1070-89	Lanfranc, archbishop, statesman and church builder
1070-77	Cathedral rebuilt by Archbishop Lanfranc
1093-1109	St Anselm, archbishop; reconstruction of the Quire begun
1130	Consecration of Anselm's quire
1162	St Thomas, archbishop
1170	St Thomas murdered 29 December
1174	Anselm's quire destroyed by fire, 5 September
1175	Complete rebuilding of the quire begun by William of Sens
1178	William of Sens injured; work taken over by William the Englishman
1184	Quire completed (as it now exists)
1184-90	Baldwin, archbishop
1207-13	Canterbury monks exiled by King John
1220	Translation of St Thomas's remains to the shrine in the Trinity Chapel
1234-45	St Edmund, archbishop
1376	Death of the Black Prince (tomb in the Trinity Chapel)
1377	Demolition of the old Romanesque nave; existing nave begun Great Cloister reconstructed

Crypt: carved capital, late 11th century.

1405	Existing nave completed
1413	Death of Henry IV (tomb in Trinity Chapel with Joan of Navarre d. 1437)
1424-34	South-west tower built
1468	West transept completed
1498	Bell Harry Tower completed
1517	Completion of the Christ Church gateway
1538	Spoliation of Becket's shrine
	Demolition of St Augustine's Abbey
1540	Dissolution of Christ Church Priory by Henry VIII
1541	Dean and Chapter incorporated by royal charter
	Nicholas Wotton, first dean (-1567)
	The King's School granted a charter by Henry VIII
1556-58	Reginald Pole, last Roman Catholic Archbishop of Canterbury
1633-45	William Laud, archbishop (executed 1645)
1642-48	Civil War: destruction of monuments, glass, etc
1660	Restoration of the Cathedral begun
1682	Return stalls in the quire commissioned
1832	Lanfranc's north-west tower finally replaced by a matching copy of the south-west tower

Chapter 1

The Building of the Cathedral to 1200

On Whitsunday 597 King Ethelbert of Kent was baptized by St Augustine in the Christian Faith. The act was symbolic as the first official acceptance of Christianity by any of the various rulers in the Anglo-Saxon kingdoms, and it is appropriate that Canterbury Cathedral should today be respected as the mother church of the Anglican Communion and its archbishops enthroned in St Augustine's chair. There had been Christians here in Roman times, when the town was Durovernum, tribal capital of the Cantii, and the earliest cathedral was probably an existing church building, rehallowed by Augustine in 602 and dedicated to Christ Jesus the Saviour. Some 150 years later, Archbishop Cuthbert added a second building (no longer existing) to the east, intended both as a baptistry and for the burial of subsequent archbishops.

In 1011 Canterbury was added to the innumerable English towns which had suffered attack from marauding Danes, who swept up the rivers, burning and pillaging from their longships. The city was sacked, the Cathedral Church was set on fire, and of the clergy who had taken refuge there only four escaped. Alphege, the archbishop, was hauled off to the Danish camp at Greenwich as a likely source of ransom. Refusing to let others suffer financial hardship for his sake, he was set up as a target at which drunken Danes shied the oxbones left over from their feasting, and was pelted to death. Later canonized, he joined Archbishops Dunstan and Thomas Becket in a trinity of Canterbury saints venerated by medieval pilgrims.

A year after the Norman Conquest of England in 1066, the old cathedral was wrecked beyond repair by a disastrous fire which broke out in the city. When Lanfranc, first of the Norman archbishops, was consecrated at Canterbury in 1070, the ceremony had to be held in an improvised shelter close to the Saxon ruins.

One of Canterbury's finest churchmen, and the first to assert her primacy above the province of York, Lanfranc took in hand a complete reorganization of the monastery (see chapter 2) and began at once to rebuild the Cathedral. As abbot of St Etienne at Caen in Normandy he had supervised the reconstruction of the abbey church there, and the influence of the earlier building, which stands today, is still traceable in the English Cathedral. The new Romanesque building, consisting of an imposing

Lanfranc's name scratched, on the wall of St Martin's Chapel to mark where his remains were translated after the fire of 1174.

Quire screen (mid 15th century): King Ethelbert of Kent holding the Saxon cathedral.

Stairs and doorway to the crypt - early 12th century (Anselm's reconstruction).

The Accord of Winchester, 1072. The document first asserted the primacy of the province of Canterbury over York (the archbishops becoming, by a happy compromise, Primate of All England and Primate of England respectively). At the bottom are the crosses of William the Conqueror and Queen Matilda (neither of whom could write), the signatures of Lanfranc and other bishops with the formal 'Ego subscripsi' (I assent), and the signature of the Archbishop of York who wrote 'Ego concedo' (I concede).

Seal of Christ Church Priory, 1104. The first seal after the Norman Conquest, showing the church in a primitive state.

nave with a fine west front and a sanctuary at its eastern end, was dedicated in October, 1077.

It is something of a paradox, however, that most of the Romanesque work now remaining in the Cathedral belongs to the period, not of the vigorous and energetic Lanfranc, but of his successor, a man quite as admirable but very different in character. Four years during which the revenues of the see were appropriated by the degenerate King William Rufus were followed in 1093 by the appointment of Anselm as archbishop. Wise and saintly, Anselm was a scholar of international repute. It is to his vision, and to the enthusiasm of the monastery's priors Ernulf and Conrad, that we owe the little staircase towers abutting the two eastern transepts, so reminiscent of the campaniles of Anselm's native Lombardy; also the cathedral treasury with its graceful bands of arcading, and the tremendous crypt, biggest of its period in England and preserved almost intact. As well as the traces of contemporary wall painting which survive in St Gabriel's Chapel, it is worth noting here the extraordinary verve and

Staircase tower, south-east transept, early 12th century (begun by Anselm, the upper tiers added a little later).

The naming of St John the Baptist: Romanesque wall painting in St Gabriel's Chapel, c.1130.

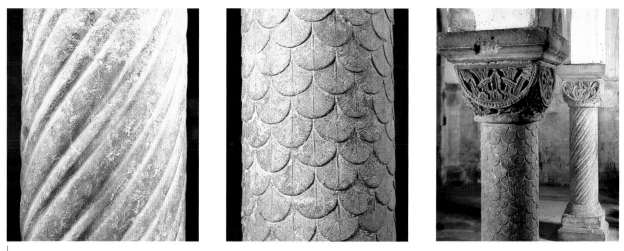

Romanesque capitals and columns in the crypt and its chapels.

The ambulatory of the Romanesque crypt, showing one of the massive columns reused from the old burnt-out quire to support the weight of the new quire above.

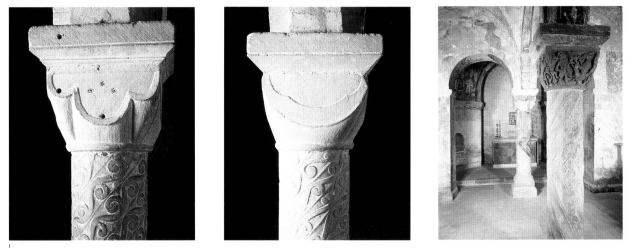

Romanesque capitals and columns in the crypt and its chapels.

Crypt: Chapel of Our Lady Undercroft, with 14th-century stone screens.

Late 12th-century vaulting in the Trinity Chapel crypt.

Seal of Christ Church Priory, 1161, showing the cathedral as it was after Anselm's reconstruction and before the great fire of 1174.

variety of the carved capitals and decorated columns throughout, an entrancing display of early twelfth-century sculpture, with evident allusion to Italy, Byzantium and the Muslim East. Some of the best of this is to be found in the Chapel of the Holy Innocents.

Above the crypt rose an extensive quire, bigger even than Lanfranc's nave, with room for seven new altars, and making an immediate impact on contemporary worshippers by its bright well-lit interior. Though the master mason was a Saxon called Blitherus, the design may well have come from Prior Ernulf himself. Consecrated in 1130, twenty-one years after Anselm's death, the splendid new quire was to last scarcely four decades before its destruction by fire on 5 September 1174.

Faced once again with the work of reconstruction, the monks were determined to appoint a truly talented and inventive architect, and intriguing evidence of their efforts in this respect may survive in the south quire ambulatory, where a single pointed arch contrasts noticeably with the round-headed arcading beside it. This was perhaps a sample of

Quire: view of the triforium and clerestory windows, 1175-9, by William of Sens.

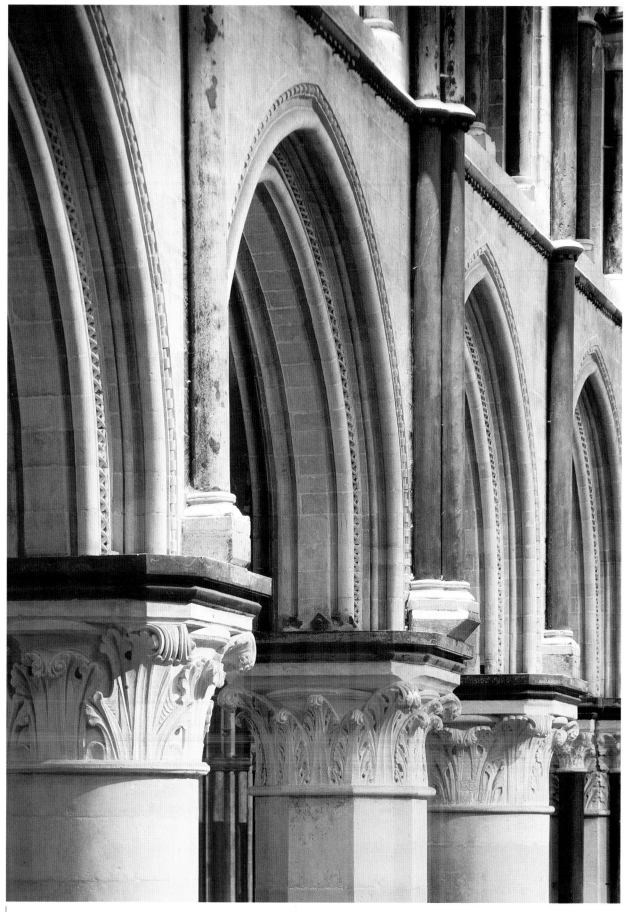

Quire: the lower arcade, with acanthus leaf capitals and Purbeck marble shafts.

South-east transept: Romanesque apses and decorative arches, early 12th century.

Romanesque arcading on the wall of the south-east transept (Anselm's reconstruction).

South quire aisle. Transitional pointed arch in round-headed Romanesque arcading, believed to be the example of the new style submitted by William of Sens to the Canterbury monks in 1174.

the new style demonstrated to the Canterbury monks by the man they eventually chose as their master builder, the Frenchman, William of Sens. A complete rebuilding of the quire began from the west end in 1175 and the various innovative features, striking for their period, were a major influence on styles employed in other English cathedrals.

The high roof rests on vaults springing from a clerestory above triforia with clustered columns, whose decorated capitals reflect the carving on those of the great pillars of the aisles below. Not only are these pillars much taller and more slender than any in earlier Romanesque churches, but they also support the black shafts of Purbeck marble whose explicit colour contrast was to prove so popular with designers during the great wave of cathedral building which swept across England in the following century (see, for example, Salisbury Cathedral or the quire at Worcester).

In 1178, after completing the quire transepts and while he was working on the high vault over the east transept crossing, William fell from a piece of faulty scaffolding and was permanently injured. He was to die in

The Trinity Chapel and Corona from the south east.

The Eastern Crypt, built by William the Englishman to support the new Trinity Chapel above.

France in 1180, having pioneered at Canterbury one of the earliest examples of what we now call the Gothic style. His chief assistant, ready to carry the work forward, was known as William the Englishman, 'small in body, but in workmanship of many kinds acute and honest', and it was he who rounded off the quire with the Trinity Chapel (or retro-quire in architectural terms), and the remarkable circular chamber at its furthest eastern end known as the Corona (see p21). The name derives from the relic of St Thomas's head formerly preserved here, but the effects of depth and distance created by the addition of this chapel are in any case a fitting crown to the two architects' great work, completed by 1184. Below, at the same time, the crypt had been extended and a special watching chamber created for monks to survey the pilgrims who came to St Thomas's tomb. Visually refreshing and surprising, the Canterbury Quire ranks among the foremost statements of Early English Gothic, a magnificent close to the first period in the story of the building of the Cathedral.

The quire, showing the work of William of Sens completed, beyond the transepts, by William the Englishman. Notice the curious narrowing effect before the Trinity Chapel, imposed on the designers by the remains of Anselm's ruined building.

Chapter 2 The Cathedral Priory of Christ Church

The full style of Canterbury Cathedral is the Cathedral & Metropolitical Church of Christ, Canterbury, and the great Benedictine Priory, whose monks staffed the Cathedral for 550 years, bore the same dedication. St Augustine, the first Archbishop, was a follower of the Benedictine Rule, and Gregory the Great, the Pope who inspired his mission to the Saxons in 597, was a disciple of Benedict himself. Following the Benedictine revival in England during the early eleventh century, initiated by Archbishop Dunstan, and the reforms set in motion by Lanfranc after the Norman conquest, the organisation of Christ Church became typical of that of most other large monastic houses of medieval England.

At the head of the community was the Prior, nominated by vote of the monks in the chapter house and exercising wide and substantial authority. His role, essentially a local one, was quite distinct from that of the bishop or archbishop, whose broader responsibilities embraced a very much larger number of churches and clergy throughout the diocese and, in the case of Canterbury, the religious life of the entire country above that. Nevertheless, Canterbury's priors, as befitted a monastery of such size and wealth, were given special privileges by the popes, including the wearing of a mitre, and generally they seem to have been men well worthy of their office.

Other monastic officials, the Precentor, the Sacrist, the Cellarer and the Chamberlain, were in charge of the various spheres of daily life in the priory and the cathedral. A medieval monastery such as Christ Church was an immense diversified concern, a centre for prayer, meditation and study, a school, a focus for music, painting and fine craftsmanship, a purveyor of all kinds of hospitality and a great landholder. Each of these departments needed its team of monks with their appropriate superior. The Precentor, for example, not only supervised musical activity but also looked after the library and coached the novices. The Sacrist saw to the upkeep of the Cathedral fabric and furnishings, and took charge of the vital supply of candles and wax lights which blazed before every shrine and altar in the church.

To the Cellarer was given the job of providing the food and drink, not only for the monks but for the scores of guests, rich and poor, entertained by the monastery. He had to tour the Priory's farms, ensuring constant supplies of corn and meat, fuel for heating and timber for repairs.

Illuminated letter R from the *Legenda Sanctorum* typical of the Canterbury *scriptorium* of the early 12th century.

Part of a contemporary copy of the Domesday Book of Christ Church, Canterbury, c. 1100.

The Great Cloister, completed in 1414 by Stephen Lote.

12th-century chalice and paten in silver gilt, found in the tomb of Archbishop Hubert Walter.

The chamberlain's job was to look after the clothing, laundry and sleeping arrangements, as well as regular shaving and washing by the monks. Every three weeks the monkish tonsures were shaved, and on Saturday nights there was a general foot bath. Full bathing was compulsory at Christmas, optional on other occasions.

The monks seem always to have lived well, and the monastic estates, ably managed, furnished a lavish table. Dining at Canterbury during the twelfth century, the prolific Welsh writer Gerald de Barri, 'Giraldus Cambrensis', says that he saw sixteen dishes of spiced meats set before the prior and his guests. Archbishop Thomas's patron Archbishop Theobald, taking temporary charge of the Priory's financial administration, angered the community by urging them to retrench on hospitality.

More serious discord between priors and archbishops arose partly from this very issue. During the archiepiscopate immediately succeeding Theobald, that of Becket himself, conflict was in fact focused in other directions (see chapter 3), but the old friction returned with the consecration of Archbishop Baldwin in 1184. Baldwin, a monk of the ascetic Cistercian order, was duly shocked by the wealth of choice food given as Christmas and Easter presents to the monastery, and his attempts to check the custom were among several features of a relationship which, from being precarious. became wholly catastrophic. His election was in any case strongly objected to by the Prior, who had actually fainted during an argument over the issue with the king, Henry II, and been revived by the anxious monarch dashing water in his face and crying 'Take heart, my lord Prior, I spoke only in jest, take heart and be merry'.

Saxon pocket sundial (10th century) found in the cloisters in 1938. The months are arranged in pairs, six on either side of the sundial, with two spots marked on each. Insert the pin in the hole appropriate to the month and hang the sundial facing the sun: the shadow of the pin will reach the lower spot at 12 noon, the upper at 9 am and 3 pm. These are the hours of tierce, sext and nones, the monks' offices during the working day.

When Archbishop Hubert Walter's tomb was opened in 1890 some of the garments in which he had been buried in July 1205 were found intact after nearly 700 years - including this one of a pair of buskins. Permission to wear buskins was granted by the Pope to the Archbishop in the 12th-century. The buskin, made in one piece with a heel constructed like a knitted sock, was held up by laces crossed behind the knee and tied above

Merriment was scarcely in order when Baldwin announced his intention of founding a college of seventy canons at Hackington, outside Canterbury, in an obvious bid to override the Priory's ancient rights as the electoral college for the appointment of the archbishop. The quarrel was taken to Rome and dragged on for six years, the issue growing heavily political as the King of France sided with the monks while King Henry took Baldwin's part. Baldwin himself, with a sort of dogged ineptitude, made a tactless gesture in naming as monastic Cellarer and then Prior the egregious Roger Norreys, a drunken profligate later to be inflicted as Abbot on the unfortunate monks of Evesham.

After a form of siege, during which the monks were supplied with food by the citizens, and the Canterbury Jews prayed for them in their synagogue, a reconciliation was effected by King Richard I in 1189. Baldwin tried to refound the Hackington college at his newly acquired manor of Lambeth (where today's Archbishops still live) and the struggle was carried on by his

The unique Romanesque staircase in the Green Court, c. 1153, leading to the heavily rebuilt remnant of the North Hall, in which lay pilgrims were given lodging just inside the priory gate.

immensely gifted successor Hubert Walter, Justiciar under Richard I and the creator of an early system of magistrates. But papal intervention finally prevailed, the collegiate scheme was abandoned and the Priory given a merely nominal right in the election of further primates - similar to that enjoyed to this day by English cathedral chapters.

For a last time the monks tried to influence events when they gave their support to Pope Innocent III's choice of his friend Stephen Langton to fill Hubert's place in 1205. For this they were exiled for six years by the infuriated King John, while the Pope retaliated by placing England under an interdict, and the quarrel was at last patched up with Langton's enthronement in 1213.

From this early period of Christ Church's history extensive traces still survive of the domestic buildings of the monastery. Beyond the cloister are the remains of Lanfranc's dormitory for the monks and at right angles to it the *reredorter*, a large lavatory, with seven arches still existing on which the seats were originally supported. Opposite, in the infirmary cloister, is the magnificent cone-capped water tower, with brick buttresses and ogival windows added later, built as part of a general programme of improvements by Prior Wibert.

View of the Cathedral from the north, looking across the site of the main monastic buildings of the 11th and 12th centuries. The refectory and kitchens lay to the right in this picture, the dormitories in the centre (with Wibert's water tower just visible in the infirmary cloister beyond), and the infirmary hall and chapel out of the picture to the left.

Remains of the undercroft of the dormitory, built by Lanfranc to sleep up to 150 monks.

St Paul at Miletus, shaking off the viper. A 12th-century wall painting in St Anselm's Chapel.

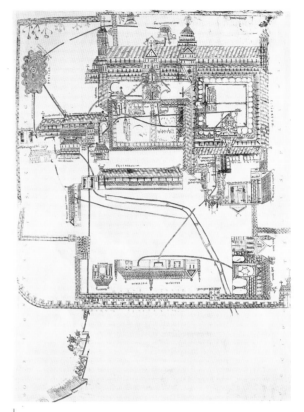

The drainage and water supply system of Christ Church Priory, from a 12th-century drawing (original at Trinity College, Cambridge).

Wibert, Prior for 14 years from 1153, provided the splendid monastic water supply, of which a unique contemporary diagram exists. 'Among his many other good works,' says the Priory register. 'was the aquaduct of this church which he had made, with pools, wash basins and bowls.' From springs north east of the cathedral the water was taken to a conduit house, thence through the city wall and over ground belonging to the canons of St Gregory's Priory, who gave the Christ Church monks a yearly basket of good apples in return for use of the supply. In the water tower the water was sent up brass pipes to a cistern on the first storey, where the monks could wash. Wibert also devised a system for flushing the drains, using rain water from the gutters on the cathedral roof.

Other features of Wibert's building programme included the imposing Green Court gateway and the handsome romanesque staircase formerly leading to a hall built during the same period. East of the water tower are Lanfranc's treasury or *vestiarium*, and the ruined arcades of the twelfth-century infirmary and beyond these, incorporated in a house east of the cathedral itself, lies the monastic guest house known as Master, or Meister, Omers, after a thirteenth-century Priory official.

Prior Wibert's water tower, on the north-east side of the Cathedral.

Within the cathedral itself is further evidence, however tantalizingly sparse, of the monks' activity as craftsmen. Notice, for example, high up on the north-east wall of St Anselm's Chapel, the painted mural panel showing St Paul shaking off the viper at Miletus, twelfth-century work, with suggestions, in the pose of the saint and the folds of his robes, of similar figures in the Byzantine mosaics of Norman Sicily. An Italian influence can perhaps also be traced in the series of inlaid marble roundels in the pavement of the Trinity Chapel, showing the signs of the zodiac, the months of the year and the virtues and vices. These were originally laid down as an embellishment to Becket's shrine in the early thirteenth century, and therefore date from the period immediately following the monks' exile at St Omer in France. There may also be some influence here through Archbishop Stephen Langton, who had been in Rome as a cardinal until 1213, and must have seen everywhere the work of the Cosmati family in this style.

South wall and chancel arch of the ruined infirmary chapel.

Of the Priors of the later Middle Ages three in particular stand out as enterprising builders and capable and admired superiors of the Christ Church community. In 1285 Henry of Eastry was elected Prior. Under his guidance the Priory reached the highest point of its prosperity: he not only succeeded in clearing it of debts amounting to about half a million pounds in modern money, but also enriched the Cathedral and the monastery precincts with a wealth of new building, including a new brewery on the north side of the Green Court, the lower levels of the chapter house, with stalls for the monks and a seat of honour for the Prior, and the fine stone screen which encloses three sides of the quire stalls in the Cathedral itself. Robert Hathbrand, Prior from 1338 to 1370, as well as redesigning the Black Prince's chantry in the crypt (now the Huguenots' Chapel, see chapter 6) added a new refectory to the infirmary, the Table Hall which survives as the Cathedral choir house, and remodelled its chapel, ruins of whose chancel, with its Decorated arches and windows, still remain. It was he who also first proposed the rebuilding of the nave.

Prior Henry of Eastry, carved stone effigy in the south quire aisle, 1331. A tough and forbidding figure, particularly in old age, Eastry's priorate lasted a record forty-six years: he died while celebrating mass, and is the only Prior to have been buried in a full tomb in the cathedral.

Inlaid marble roundels in the floor of the Trinity Chapel (originally in front of the shrine of St Thomas).

Boss in the vaulting of the cloister thought to depict the head of Henry Yevele, designer of the nave and master of Stephen Lote, designer of the Great Cloister.

Greatest of the three was undoubtedly Thomas Chillenden, whose twenty-year priorate from 1391 amply justified his contemporary accolade 'Flower of English Priors, worthy to be glorified for his good works'. His extensive additions to the conventual buildings included a magnificent new wagon-vaulted roof to the chapter house and the complete reconstruction of the Great Cloister. In both cases the architect was probably Stephen Lote, a Kentish pupil of Henry Yevele, designer of the nave, which was also completed in Chillenden's priorate (see chapter 4). The cloister is another outstanding example of early Perpendicular work, with its four-light windows capped by crocketed ogee gables and typical sprays of fan tracery. Like the chapter house it boasts a wealth of detailed heraldry in the bosses of its lierne vaults. The doorway in the north-west corner gave entrance to the Cellarer's lodging and still has, beside it, the serving hatch where bread and beer were given not, for example, to monks returning from journeys between meal times.

Like other monastic houses the Priory ultimately fell victim to King Henry VIII's wholesale spoliation during the 1530s. After visits by the royal commissioners and the plunder of many Cathedral treasures, the monastery was formally surrendered by its inmates in 1540. Of its 53 monks, twenty-eight became members of the new cathedral foundation, and the others, including Prior Thomas Goldwell, were pensioned off.

The early 15th-century roof of the chapter house.

Chapter 3 Saint Thomas Becket

The development of Canterbury as one of the world's great religious centres is linked inextricably with the martyrdom and subsequent canonization of its most famous archbishop - Saint Thomas Becket. Without the shrine of St Thomas, the continuing flow of pilgrims to the medieval city, and the involved tissue of legend and hard fact into which early biographers wove the martyr's life, the mother church of England, for all its other associations, might well have been just another cathedral. Even today, when many different interests draw visitors to the building, its ancient fame as the resting place of a great English saint endures.

Poetry, novels, drama and film have all celebrated the conflict between the archbishop and his former friend and master King Henry II. From the Icelandic *Saga of Archbishop Thomas* to Tennyson's portentous late Victorian tragedy *Becket* and T. S. Eliot's *Murder In The Cathedral*, that most intricately-wrought of modern verse dramas, writers have responded to the romance and heroism implicit in the story of one man's firm defiance of absolute authority. Thomas has been presented as a champion of oppressed Saxons against Normans, as a stalwart defender of church liberties and as a man agonized by the need to choose between worldly advancement and spiritual recompense. The facts are altogether less simple and more interesting, and make the head-on collision between king and archbishop seem as inevitable in a personal sense as it was in a political context.

Thomas Becket was born in London on 21 December 1118. His father, Gilbert Becket, was a prosperous merchant who had held office as sheriff of the city, and his mother Matilda (discounting the charming legend which makes her out to have been the daughter of a Saracen emir) came from Caen in Normandy. 'Quick of learning, keen of memory and clear of understanding in all things' Thomas was sent to school at Merton Priory in Surrey, where he would have acquired the basic education of a medieval 'clerk' - grammar, logic, rhetoric and a thorough knowledge of Latin. This does not imply that he was already intended for the church, since literacy was in demand among professional men of his own class and among the nobility. A fondness for study, however, sent him on to the famous schools of Paris, then the best in Europe, where he may have attended lectures by the great Peter Abelard.

It was at this time that his thoughts seem to have turned towards an

Seal of Archbishop Theobald, Becket's patron, probably c. 1155. The archbishop is in full pontificals and holds a simple crosier.

Book of Hours of the Blessed Virgin Mary (late 15th century).

St Thomas Becket. 13th-century stained glass panel (Trinity Chapel, north aisle).

Thomas kneeling before an altar, with a monk in attendance (c. 1220, Trinity Chapel, north aisle).

ecclesiastical career, and the vow of chastity which he took in Paris against the background of an unruly student life suggests that he had begun to consider his future seriously. Returning to England in 1140, after five years in France, he eventually joined the staff of Theobald, Archbishop of Canterbury, who soon despatched him for further study in canon and civil law to the renowned faculties of Bologna and Auxerre.

Thomas's evident administrative skill was given every encouragement by the Archbishop, who made him Archdeacon of Canterbury. and his progress during the turbulent reign of King Stephen, a time when 'Christ and his saints slept', was noted with interest and envy by others. In 1154 Stephen died, having already willed his crown to the son of his cousin Matilda, with whom he had fought inconclusively for twenty years. The new king, twenty-one-year old Henry of Anjou, crowned as Henry II, was to prove one of the most colourful, decisive and memorable of England's medieval rulers.

It was Theobald who recommended Thomas Becket to Henry as Chancellor of the Realm. This meant not only that he was entrusted with one of the highest offices of state, in which he could gain first-hand experience of the continuing problem of maintaining a balance between the various sectors of the community, but also that he was brought into close personal contact with the king. The two men took an instant liking to each other, and their mutual respect was evidently based on certain traits of character common to both: a readiness to act quickly and

Henry II and Thomas during a moment of reconciliation (c. 1220, Trinity Chapel, north aisle).

firmly, a determination to stand by decisions once made, a hot temper and a refusal to mince words. (We can find an interesting illustration of this in the coarse expression - 'you pimp!' - with which Thomas addressed FitzUrse, one of his four assailants, a few minutes before his own murder).

Diplomat, mediator, advisor, administrator - it must have seemed, at the time of Archbishop Theobald's death in 1161, as if Thomas were truly the king's man. It was surely no haphazard choice which led Henry a year later to fix on so close a friend to fill the vacant see. But Thomas, surprisingly from a modern point of view, was still only a clerk in minor orders; he was ordained priest on 2 June 1162, consecrated bishop on the following morning and enthroned as Archbishop in Canterbury Cathedral on the same day. In assuming his new office he had taken the most momentous step of his career and set himself on a fatal course as far as his relationship with the king was concerned.

Relations between Church and State were one of the fundamental causes of political unrest during the Middle Ages. Henry's great-uncle William Rufus had quarrelled with the church, and so (as we have already seen) would his son John over the appointment of a later Archbishop of Canterbury. Nowadays we may find it hard to sympathize with Thomas's intransigent attitude, so obviously stiffened by pride and by a resolve, in the best traditions of powerful prelates, to uphold the dignity and privileges of his office to the utmost. The most notorious example of this

Three mailed knights at the cathedral door (c. 1220, Trinity Chapel, north aisle).

An armed knight, with a distraught monk, apparently inside the cathedral (c. 1220, Trinity Chapel, north aisle).

is his sustained condemnation, during a sermon at Canterbury, of a man who had docked the tail of a horse belonging to one of the archiepiscopal servants. Of one outstanding quality we can have no doubt, however. What he did was done with complete conviction that it was right, and with untiring devotion to the church and the faith he served.

Thomas's main contention with Henry, apart from those over the disposal of church property and the application of taxes, concerned the issue of how churchmen should be tried and punished under the law. The king's interest in improving the antiquated English legal mechanism was well known, and it was during his reign that the jury system, now in use throughout the world, was introduced for the first time. Royal courts could still apply a range of harsh penalties, including various forms of mutilation, and it was natural enough that the clergy should wish to be tried by their own courts, where milder punishments were given. In 1164 Henry promulgated the Constitutions of Clarendon, a series of sixteen clauses clarifying the relationship of Church to State and asserting the judicial rights of the crown. To these Thomas at first agreed, then withdrew his assent, accompanying this retraction with a symbolic act of penance which, under the circumstances, can only have been seen as an overt criticism of the king's reforms.

The rift between king and Archbishop was now complete. Summoning Thomas to Northampton, Henry called on him to account for the money he had been given to spend as Chancellor of England and for the revenues of the bishoprics and abbacies he had held. Angry scenes ensued, during which Gilbert Foliot, Bishop of London, actually tried to wrench Thomas's primatial cross from his hands, and Thomas later compared himself to the martyr St Stephen. Despite his enemies in the church and among Henry's followers, he was already a popular hero with the common people and many of the clergy, and when he finally fled from Northampton on a stormy October night in 1164 he found willing helpers to speed him on his way to France.

The murder of Becket: a reconstruction, by Professor E.W. Tristram, of the 15th-century painting at the head of the tomb of Henry IV and Joan of Navarre.

Site of the martyrdom of St Thomas Becket in the north-west transept

He stayed in exile for six years, first at the Cistercian Abbey of Pontigny, then at Sens, always with the support of the King of France. There was no question, during this period, of his relinquishing his pastoral responsibility, and in 1169 he excommunicated the Bishops of London and Salisbury, at the same time threatening England with an interdict - the total suppression of all rites and sacraments of the church. In 1170 he came back to England at last, landing at the port or Sandwich in his own diocese, to be greeted by cheering crowds lining the route to Canterbury itself, where music and feasting celebrated his return.

In the Cathedral, where he preached on the text 'Here have we no abiding city, but we seek one to come', it seemed to the monks 'as if his heart burned within his very countenance'. Hardened in resolve, refusing to compromise, he was clearly ready to die for what he believed in. It was his bitterest foe, Archbishop Roger of York, who touched off the explosion of rage which was ultimately to lead to Becket's martyrdom. At an audience with Henry at Bures in Normandy, Roger had said: 'While Thomas lives, you will have neither quiet times nor a tranquil kingdom', whereupon the king, flying into one of his customary rages, cried, 'Who will rid me of this low-born (some say 'turbulent') priest?'

Four knights, Richard Brito, Hugh de Moreville, Reginald FitzUrse and William de Tracy, chose, for mixed personal and political motives, to take Henry at his word and set off for England. Mustering followers, they arrived at Canterbury on 29 December 1170. An interview with Thomas followed the usual pattern of accusations and angry rebuttals from either side,

Adam the Forester shot by a poacher. A scene from one of the 13th-century Miracle windows (Trinity Chapel, south aisle).

and as the knights and their men gathered around the palace with cries of 'Reaux, reaux', 'King's men, king's men', Thomas was persuaded by the monks to enter the Cathedral, though he insisted the door should be left unbarred. The knights burst into the building as Thomas was hustled through the north-west transept, while the late afternoon service of vespers was in progress. In the darkness they called out for the archbishop, and Thomas came down to face them. They tried to seize hold of him, but Thomas, scornful and insulting, shook them off, actually throwing FitzUrse to the ground.

It was FitzUrse himself who threatened the Archbishop with his drawn sword. Tracy, calling 'Strike, strike!' to the others, cut deeply into the martyr's head, and it was only at a third blow that he staggered to the ground, calling on an earlier Canterbury martyr St Alphege and murmuring 'For the name of Jesus and the defence of the church I am willing to die' as Richard Brito gave the death stroke. The force of this blow was such as to cut off the crown of the head and shatter the tip of the blade on the stone pavement - hence the name given to the nearby altar of the Sword's Point, on which the tip of the sword was placed for the veneration of posterity. This altar, destroyed in 1538, was restored in 1986.

The site of the martyrdom is preserved today in the north-west transept. Within hours of the Archbishop's death, and to the accompaniment of a violent storm, the Cathedral was thronged with a mourning crowd, and two days later began the series of miracles which, in 1173, was to warrant his canonization 'among the company of martyrs' by Pope Alexander III.

Several of these miracles, as well as episodes from Thomas's life, are commemorated in the series of stained glass windows, prabably the most enjoyable of all the windows at Canterbury,

Plague in the house of Sir Jordan Fitz-eisulf (c. 1220, Trinity Chapel, north aisle). Bottom left: 1, the funeral of the first victim, the nurse Britonis; 2, Sir Jordan's younger son dying before his parents' eyes; 3, holy water from St Thomas is poured into his mouth. Top row right: 4, Sir Jordan promises a thank offering of money for his son's recovery; 5, the boy's parents give thanks; 6, St Thomas appears in a dream to the blind beggar, Gimp, and bids him warn Sir Jordan. Middle row: 7, from his bed, Gimp passes on the warning; 8, this being ignored, other members of the household are stricken and Sir Jordan's elder son dies; 9, Sir Jordan, accompanied by his wife and younger son, accomplishes his vow at the tomb of St Thomas.

Pilgrims at the shrine of St Thomas (after 1220, Trinity Chapel, south aisle). Both pictures show the gold-plated chest standing on round arches supported by slender marble columns.

From the story of Rodbertus of Rochester (from the Miracle windows, Trinity Chapel, north aisle). Notice the fat green frogs on the river bank.

Henry II doing penance at the tomb of St Thomas in 1174 (c. 1220, Trinity Chapel, north aisle).

which were placed in the aisles of the newly constructed Trinity Chapel in the early thirteenth century. Eight of the original twelve survive, and all are delightfully vivid in their range of colours, and lively and energetic in their approach to composition. The association of Thomas with the common people becomes apparent in such episodes as that of Adam the Forester, who was shot by a poacher and recovered after drinking the miraculous water of St Thomas, or the story of William Kellett the carpenter, who cut his leg on a work bench, prayed to the saint, who appeared to him in a dream, and awoke to find his leg restored whole.

Children also figure in these hagiographical episodes. In one series we see little Geoffrey of Winchester, saved first from a fever and then from a falling building. The children of Sir Jordan Fitz-eisulf (in fact a personal friend of Thomas's) fall ill; St Thomas is called upon to heal them. One son, near death, is saved, but the parents fail to give due thanks to Thomas. A blind cripple is sent to warn Sir Jordan, who ignores the advice, whereupon another child actually dies and the repentant father lavishes gifts on the martyr's tomb. Note also the tale of Rodbertus (Robert) of Rochester, the naughty boy who played truant from school to go and throw stones at frogs in the River Medway. He slipped in the mud and fell into the river but, with a mixture of the saint's blood and holy water, was brought to life once more. The essential humanity of the inspired artist who created this series is brought out in small details, such as the fat green frogs, the other boys running home to tell Robert's mother, and the shattered parents watching as their son's body is fished from the river by a man with a hook.

In three of these pictures the shrine of St Thomas is depicted, and in many others the tomb in which the saint had originally been buried. Immediately after the murder the body was in fact placed in an iron chest, which lay within a wooden coffin decked with jewels and votive offerings, encased in a marble tomb in the eastern crypt, and it was to this tomb that Henry II came, most notable among early pilgrims, in July 1174. His elaborate penance included a barefoot walk through the city and culminated in flagellation by the Prior and all eighty monks of Christ Church Priory. Only six weeks after this occasion came the fire which gutted Anselm's glorious new choir - and the peculiar design of the structure erected to take its place (with its

The site of St Thomas's shrine in the Trinity Chapel from 1220 until its destruction in 1538.

extended retro-quire and Corona) was largely dictated by the need to provide St Thomas with a worthy shrine, and was, of course, paid for out of funds provided by the pilgrims who were already flocking to the city in his honour. The shrine, in the new Trinity Chapel, was eventually completed after the return of the Canterbury monks from their exile in France and the enthronement of Stephen Langton as archbishop on 7 July 1220, to mark the fiftieth anniversary of Thomas's martyrdom, his remains were translated from the crypt to their new resting place in the presence of King Henry III, the papal legate Pandulf, and all the bishops and abbots of England.

Pilgrimage provided continuing revenue for Canterbury throughout the Middle Ages, and this of course forms the narrative framework of Geoffrey Chaucer's *Canterbury Tales*. The Pilgrims' Way is still easily traceable in its course across the south of England from Winchester,

Vaulting of the Trinity Chapel, showing the boss over the shrine of St Thomas from which the pulley to raise the wooden cover of the tomb chest was suspended.

and the word 'canter' (from 'Canterbury pace') survives as a reminder of the ambling gallop of the pilgrims who rode along it. Among other interesting survivals of pilgrimage is the name of the approach road to the city on the south-western side - 'Wincheap', meaning 'wine market', from the number of hostelries for the refreshment of the thirsty travellers. With the advent of Henry VIII, however, the situation changed dramatically. In 1538, two years before the dissolution of the Priory, the shrine was despoiled and destroyed. Cartloads of treasure were carried off and the Regale of France, the great ruby sent by Louis VII as an offering to Becket's memory, was set as a thumb ring and worn by the king himself - a symbol of the triumph of the State over the power of the Church. St Thomas's name was formally expunged from the official calendar of the English church, and little visible trace of his cult left in the Cathedral.

Nothing, however, could successfully destroy his memory, as alive in Canterbury today as it was five centuries ago. A man whose moral force and strength of character was appreciated even by his enemies, a man who inspired love and devotion among hundreds of people, from learned monks who tried vainly to protect him in his last hours to the humblest country folk who sought his blessing on his return from exile, Thomas Becket remains one of the great champions and exemplars of Christianity.

Steps to the Trinity Chapel in the south aisle, worn by the feet and knees of pilgrims.

Eastbridge Hospital, Canterbury, founded c. 1190 to afford hospitality to pilgrims and dedicated to St Thomas. This is the Undercroft in which the pilgrims slept.

Chapter 4 The Late Middle Ages

The fourteenth century saw the beginnings of the great second period of building and embellishing in the Cathedral. A series of inspired and enthusiastic archbishops and priors, and the increasing interest shown by members of the English royal house, helped to create the circumstances in which these new ventures could be set in progress and brought to completion, often with extraordinary swiftness.

Prior Robert Hathbrand we have already noted as the rebuilder of the monastic infirmary and its chapel. In 1363 he supervised the work, at the south side of the crypt, on the elegant chantry which had been founded by Edward the Black Prince in return for a papal dispensation enabling him to marry his cousin Joan Plantagenet, Countess of Kent. The chantry was to contain two altars, to the Holy Trinity and to the Virgin, with a priest for each. The chapel has the characteristic column clusters and branching lierne vaults of its period, and especially attractive are the carved bosses such as those showing the head of Joan herself, Samson with the lion, and a pious pelican nesting in an oak tree.

A more significant change in the Cathedral's appearance began in 1377, when the old Romanesque nave, by now somewhat dwarfed beside the majestic choir, was demolished and a new one designed and executed under the direction of the master mason Henry Yevele, who had already worked so effectively at Westminster Abbey. The nave, one of the most magnificent surviving examples of early Perpendicular Gothic, is noteworthy for its daring emphasis upon height and for the beauty of its masses of vertical lines, branching upwards into the sprays of rib-vaulting meeting at the long central row of gilt bosses. Twenty-eight years were needed to complete this ambitious project, with its matching windows and exterior buttresses and crockets, and the whole ensemble makes a superb architectural complement to the lofty sobriety of the Early English quire.

Prior Chillenden was in office when the nave was given its finishing touches (an average of £500 a year - considerable by medieval standards - being spent on the work) and in his programme of reconstruction and adornment he included the splendid carved pulpitum or stone screen at the top of the steps from the nave to the Quire (see p. 47). This, like the cloister, is ascribed to Stephen Lote and typifies the increasing stress on ornament in the contemporary style. It still has its full array of

The shield and gauntlets of Edward, the Black Prince, which originally hung above his tomb are now displayed in the south presbytery aisle. (The accoutrements now hanging above the tomb are replicas.)

Joan Plantagenet. A boss on the ceiling of the Black Prince's chantry, 1363.

The Quire screen, or pulpitum - mid 15th century. Priorate of Thomas Goldstone I.

The nave, designed by Henry Yevele was built over twenty-eight years and completed under Prior Chillenden in 1405.

Rib-vaulting high above the columns of Yevele's nave, early 15th century.

shield-bearing angels and the original row of six kings (left to right: Richard II, Henry V, Ethelbert, Edward the Confessor, Henry IV and Henry VI) though its original figures of Christ and the twelve apostles have long since gone.

The west transept followed the nave, the south-west arm being completed sometime after 1414, the north-west by 1468. In the former the reconstruction of St Michael's chapel produced a curious anomaly: the tomb of Stephen Langton, under the altar in the apse of the original Romanesque chapel, could not be fitted into the new design, and as a result the archbishop who presided over the signature of Magna Carta now lies with his head inside the cathedral and his feet in the precincts outside. On the north side of the building, however, the site of Thomas's martyrdom was treated with contrasting respect: so holy a place, it was felt, should be left undisturbed, and to this day the floor of the north-west transept is in fact lower than that of its southern counterpart. A comparable lack of symmetry for four centuries characterized the west end of the cathedral, where the south-west tower was rebuilt by Thomas Mapilton between 1424 and 1434, leaving Lanfranc's original Romanesque tower on the north-west corner. This lop-sided arrangement continued until 1832, when the older structure was replaced by a matching replica of Mapilton's work. The south-west porch is about contemporary with the tower above it, and was built (like the Erpingham Gate to the precincts at Norwich) to commemorate the battle of Agincourt.

The last extensive addition to the cathedral fabric was made in 1494, when Prior William Sellinge, with encouragement from Cardinal Archbishop Morton, commissioned John Wastell to

Water-colour of the cathedral by James Malton (1799), before the demolition of Lanfranc's north-west tower. Notice also the absence of statues in the south-west porch.

The Bell Harry tower, crowning glory of the cathedral, by John Wastell, completed in 1498.

Detail of the south-west porch and tower, 1424-34, by Thomas Mapilton.

complete the Bell Harry tower, the dominant central feature of the church, especially when seen from a distance. The name derives, not from either of the contemporary Tudor kings, but from Prior Henry of Eastry, who had given a bell to be hung in the original tower over a hundred years before. The new tower had all the distinguishing marks of its period, including the lantern pinnacles and the tall ogival lower windows. High up inside it, under the vault (see p. 52) over the crossing between nave, transepts and choir, can be seen the fan tracery which is almost a late Perpendicular trademark. Apart from the Christ Church Gate, begun in 1507, this was the only major piece of the cathedral building to be undertaken between the accession of Henry VII and the dissolution of the Priory.

Canterbury is rich in fine monuments of all periods, including those of Edward the Black Prince and King Henry IV. The Black Prince, eldest son of King Edward III, died on 8 June 1376. His association with Canterbury had been a close one, and it is possible that Prior Hathbrand had been his tutor. Born at Woodstock in 1330 and educated in the chivalric traditions of the late Middle Ages, Edward naturally became the symbol of England's hopes and aspirations in the prolonged wars with France. An able military leader, he was given his soubriquet possibly,

Bell Harry, inside the Crossing, showing the contrast between Yevele's early Perpendicular style and Wastell's more florid fan-vaulting of a century later.

April sunlight on clustered columns in the 14th-century nave.

Edward, the Black Prince. The famous latten effigy on the south side of the Trinity Chapel, 1376.

according to the chronicler Froissart, because of the terror he inspired with his bravery and ferocity, but not because of any suit of black armour he may have worn.

He had asked to be buried in the crypt, but national pressures and the monks' sense of decorum decreed that he be accorded suitable honour in the form of an iron railed tomb close to the shrine of St Thomas, on the south side of the Trinity Chapel. Above the effigy on its tomb chest hangs a painted tester, and over this are replicas of the surcoat, helmet, gauntlets and other accoutrements of the Prince himself (the originals are displayed in a case down the steps in the south quire aisle). In the nineteenth century, Victorian romanticism took a literal attitude to the Black Prince's memory, as a result of which the original latten effigy was carefully blackened and remained under layers of paint until it was accidentally uncovered and restored to its original glory during the early 1930s.

On the opposite side of the quire lies the Black Prince's nephew Henry IV with his second wife Joan of Navarre (see p. 56). Henry's reign, dramatized so poignantly by Shakespeare, was

Wooden effigy of Archbishop Peckham, 1292. The original silver mitre, and perhaps other adornments, were stripped off at the time of the Reformation.

a difficult one, punctuated with rebellion and religious controversy and ominously full of those political disturbances which were to reach a prolonged crisis in the Wars of the Roses. He died in 1413 and Joan, a self-indulgent and unpopular consort, in1437; the two of them are portrayed in superb alabaster carving, under a canopy painted with their royal arms. These effigies are attributed to Robert Brown, and the tomb is surrounded by high iron railings which make an interesting comparison with the near-contemporary wooden screen of Henry's chantry chapel of St Edward the Confessor, just across the aisle.

Elsewhere in this part of the Cathedral are several outstanding monuments to archbishops of the fourteenth and fifteenth centuries. As a screen dividing it from the south quire aisle, St Anselm s Chapel has the tall black marble tomb of Archbishop Simon Meopham, who died in 1333. Notice here the little figures of monks studying, carved in the spandrels. and the splendid fourteenth-century iron gates. Also on the south side are Archbishop Stratford under a stone canopy, dating from 1348, and Archbishop Kempe under a remarkable wooden one of 1454. Prior Henry of Eastry (d.1331) lies further to the west (see p. 31). The north-west transept contains the tall canopied recess holding the wooden effigy of Archbishop Peckham, originally a Franciscan friar, who died in 1292.

In the north quire aisle is the sumptuous tomb of Archbishop Henry Chichele, who died in 1443, with a canopy supported on broad piers decorated with saints. On top of the tomb chest the archbishop lies dressed in his episcopal vestments, his hands clasped in prayer. Below, a typical feature of late medieval monumental art, is the gisant or naked cadaver, embodying the

Henry IV and Joan of Navarre. Alabaster effigies on the north side of the Trinity Chapel attributed to Robert Brown, 1437.

transient quality of mortal life. Every fifty years the tomb is restored by Chichele's Oxford foundation, the College of All Souls, and is due to be done again in 1997. He was an intensely patriotic man, an ardent supporter of King Henry V, whom he had welcomed here in 1415, a few months after the Battle of Agincourt. Seven years later, following Henry's death in France, Chichele was on hand as Archbishop to receive the king's body at Dover. Soon after this he gave orders for his own tomb to be prepared. He did not die until 1443, but the tomb was probably completed by 1425, when a goldsmith named Bernard took sanctuary behind the railings, in headlong flight from a mob of enraged citizens who had chased him into the church during high mass.

Near the Chichele tomb is the later monument to Cardinal Thomas Bourchier, who, as chief ecclesiastical prop of the house of York during the Wars of the Roses, crowned King Edward IV in 1461. Bourchier (pronounced 'Bowcher') who figures in Shakespeare's Richard III, died in 1486 and was buried in this elegant marble tomb, which has evident allusions to the Chichele tomb, and some of its original figures remaining.

Other survivals from the rebuilding and refurbishing work which continued until the Christ Church monks were finally dispossessed of their monastery in the sixteenth century are displayed in the extensive wall frescos, in the north quire aisle, which show the legend of St Eustace, one of several saints to whom Christ is reputed to have appeared on a crucifix carried between the antlers of a stag, and in the filigree fan tracery of the Chapel of Our Lady Martyrdom, in the north-west transept.

15th-century carved wooden screen of the chapel of St Edward the Confessor.

Monks in the *scriptorium*. Detail from the tomb of Archbishop Meopham, 1333

The Chapel of Our Lady Martyrdom (the Dean's Chapel) fan-vaulting, c. 1460. The first on a large scale in this part of England and an interesting comparison to Wastell's later vaulting inside the Bell Harry tower.

The north quire aisle, with Chichele's tomb on the left and a glimpse of Yevele's nave in the distance.

The magnificent tomb of Archbishop Henry Chichele was probably completed by 1425 though Chichele did not die until 1443.

The Chapel of Our Lady Martyrdom (the Dean's Chapel). A 15th-century carved angel, hidden until recently by the reredos of the altar.

Chapter 5 The Stained Glass

The ancient stained glass of Canterbury Cathedral is one of the glories of medieval English art. Its miraculous survival can only make us long for the days before the Reformation when practically the entire Cathedral was glazed with windows glorifying the great figures of the Old and New Testaments and celebrating acts and moments in the lives of saints such as Thomas Becket. In fact Canterbury was luckier than many cathedrals and churches in the early sixteenth century in escaping the attacks of pious iconoclasts, and it was only the Puritan reaction immediately before and during the Civil War which brought widespread destruction to several of the ancient windows.

Much work has been done in cleaning and restoring the glass itself, to recreate as vividly as possible the brilliance, variety and liveliness of design in the original, and since the Middle Ages various panels have been shifted and reset in different parts of the church. At the west end of the nave, for example, we can see figures from the genealogical series of windows formerly in the quire. This type of picture series was very popular in medieval churches, where it was meant as a kind of visual stimulus for a largely illiterate congregation. The quire windows original-ly showed the descent of Christ from Adam and the Patriarchs and here, reset in the lower lights of the west window, the subjects include the magnificent delving Adam, a stark, vigorous example of late twelfth-cen-tury design. Above them is an array of English kings and archbishops, dating from the late fourteenth and the fifteenth century, and the colouring of these panels, cool and restrained, is in marked contrast to the primitive exuberance of the lower series.

In the north-west transept is a poignant survival of a splendid fif-teenth-century window featuring Edward IV and his queen Elizabeth Woodville, with their children, in the traditional kneeling posture of donors (see p.63). The original ensemble comprised God the Father, Christ and the Holy Spirit, the Virgin Mary 'in seven glorious appear-ances', St Thomas Becket and a group of saints, some of whom, with prophets and apostles, can now be seen in the tracery. The rest was destroyed in 1642 by Richard Culmer, a bigoted Puritan, but the whole was clearly characterized by rich colour and expansive layout. The work was perhaps by William Neve, the royal glazier, helped by a less talented assistant, and was completed by 1482.

Adam delving. A late 12th-century panel in the west window of the nave.

61

Methuselah. A panel from the south-west transept window.

South west transept. The great south window, containing some of the late 12th-century panels originally from the quire.

King Edward IV and his family, by William Neve and assistants (north-west transept, 1482).

Early medieval armature and glazing bars in a window of the Trinity Chapel.

Jonah and the whale: 13th-century panel in the Corona.

St Edward the Confessor: 15th-century panel in St Edward's Chapel.

A biblical 'coupling' sequence from the north quire aisle. The New Testament scene, in the centre, shows the infant Christ on Mary's knee, adored by the shepherds and the Magi bearing their gifts. To the right, Joseph in state with his brothers, and the Egyptian people bringing offerings of money. To the left, Solomon receiving the Queen of Sheba accompanied by three attendants on camels (c. 1200).

Another biblical parallel. To the right the three Magi, tucked into one large bed and all with their crowns on, are warned by an angel not to return to Herod. To the left Lot's wife, looks back at the burning city of Sodom and is turned to a pillar of salt (c. 1200).

A pair of windows in the north aisle of the Trinity Chapel, showing miraculous episodes connected with St Thomas Becket.

Noah, leaning out of the ark welcomes back the dove with the olive branch (north choir aisle, c. 1200).

The sower. From the Biblical windows of the north quire aisle, this is one of two panels that remain out of three on this parable (c. 1200).

The large window in the south-west transept contains twenty-four more figures from the ancestry of Jesus which originally lined the clerestory of the choir. These include the intensely compelling full-length seated Methuselah, in the lowest row, one foot raised, his left hand clutching the arm of his throne, the other stroking his patriarchal beard.

The best of the Cathedral's treasure of stained glass is to be seen in the ambulatories and chapels of the quire and Trinity Chapel. Most of these windows belong distinctly to the twelfth- and thirteenth-century French tradition exemplified so gloriously at Chartres, with which Canterbury certainly bears comparison. They were formerly arranged in definite schemes, so that it was possible to 'read' the story represented in any given series along the line of panels or up and down the individual windows. In the clerestory were the genealogy windows already noted, a total of eighty-four panels designed to culminate in Christ and the Virgin Mary. Scenes from the life of Christ filled the apse. In the quire aisles and the eastern transept were windows whose theological subjects reflected the well-loved medieval habit of pairing events in the Old and New Testaments. In the aisles of the Trinity Chapel were the beautiful series of windows, already described, portraying works and miracles of St Thomas Becket (see chapter 3). Some of the windows, incidentally, retain their original metal frame-work, and provide an intriguing source of study for those interested in the technique of applied art in the Middle Ages.

In the north quire aisle we see the remains of the Biblical 'coupling' sequence mentioned above. These are late additions to the twelfth-century scheme, and show an interesting transitional shift from Romanesque to a later style (look, for example, at the stylistic variety in the figures in the Adoration of the Magi panel). The parallels are easily seen, though now and then the panels have become somewhat muddled and the aim of the whole scheme, as a theological commentary, has thus become confused.

The spies at Eshcol. This is associated with a New Testament panel of the Crucifixion: two men represent types of Christ and Simon of Cyrene bearing the Cross to Calvary; the grapes, gathered by the spies in the land of Canaan, symbolise the wine of the Passion which Christ left as a pledge of the Promised land of heaven (early 13th century, Corona).

The Corona still holds several of its fine panels showing the principal events from Good Friday to Pentecost, foreshadowed by scenes from the Old Testament, carefully arranged in alternating shapes around the central illustrated squares as a species of commentary. Here, for example, the symbolism of the Entombment is underlined by representations of Joseph in the pit, Samson and Delilah in bed together, Jonah cast overboard from the ship, and Daniel in the lions' den. In the same window the ultimate significance of Pentecost is deepened with illustrations of Aaron and his sons being ordained priests, Christ in Glory, Moses judging the people, and Moses receiving the tables of the law.

Of later medieval glass the most interesting survivals. apart from the portrait figures in the north-west transept windows, are those in the little chantry chapel of King Henry IV in the north choir aisle, dedicated to St Edward the Confessor. Here, peering through the screen into the tiny chamber, we can appreciate the contrast in style and colour between the three surviving figures (of St Christopher, St Edward and St Catherine, all easily identifiable by their appropriate symbols and settings) and the deep toned glazing of the Miracle windows in the aisle nearby. Notice, in the Chapel of Our Lady Martyrdom, the small armorial panels, contemporary with the stonework and dating from the primacy of Cardinal Bourchier in the mid-fifteenth century.

Few of the modern windows in the cathedral can possibly be compared, in design and effect, with the total achievement of the surviving medieval glasswork. The Victorian glass is worthy but dull, and of more recent efforts only the Coronation Window in the north-west transept, a late work by that genius of twentieth-century church decoration Sir Ninian Comper, has any real quality. Erwin Bossanyi's four windows of 1956, in the south-east transept, are an interesting example of an attempt to harmonize colour surfaces and shapes with the surrounding stone and glass of the medieval cathedral.

Chapter 6 Reformation and Civil War

The Christ Church Gate to the precincts of Canterbury Cathedral symbolizes in its overall style both an end and a beginning. It was the last major piece of building work put in hand before the Reformation and it is one of the earliest English examples of a late Gothic building to incorporate Renaissance touches (in the pilasters of the entrance arches). Thus it casts a backward glance to the days of the Christ Church Priory and looks forward to the troubled later years of King Henry VIII.

Some two decades after the gate's completion in 1517, the king had replaced the ejected prior and monks with a Dean and Chapter, incorporated by royal charter in 1541. With minor changes, this foundation has remained in charge of the administration of the cathedral and its services until the present day. Besides the dean and twelve prebendaries (who, according to Archbishop Cranmer, wasted their time 'in much idleness and . . . superfluous belly cheer') there were twelve minor canons, virgers, choristers, King's Scholars, a butler, a cook, four bellringers and other officials, making a total staff of 134. Besides these, a small college of six preachers was created, which is still in existence today.

The conduct of some of the prebendaries during these early days of the reformed English church left much to be desired. The first Dean, Nicholas Wotton, was hardly a good example to his chapter, for though he was an immensely able and talented man, whose natural modesty made him refuse offers of a bishopric on grounds of temperamental unfitness, his interests lay more in politics and diplomacy than in guiding a cathedral chapter through its fledgling years. Born in 1497, he was one of the ambassadors sent by King Henry to the Duke of Cleves in 1538 to arrange the marriage with his daughter Anne, Henry's fourth wife. In 1544 he was made Archdeacon of Gloucester, and three years later he became Dean of York, holding both places in commendam with (alongside) Canterbury. His tomb is one of the finest individual works of Renaissance art in the cathedral, showing him kneeling at prayer, while an inscription above testifies to his scholarship and linguistic skills.

By careful trimming Wotton survived the brief attempt at a counter-reformation by Queen Mary (1554-8). Archbishop Cranmer was executed, his chaplain likewise, and various canons and preachers deprived of their benefices in the general effort to reinstate Catholicism. In the Corona is the simple tomb of Cardinal Reginald Pole, last Roman Catholic

The Christ Church Gate, completed in 1517, the last major piece of priory building before the Dissolution.

Monument to Dean Nicholas Wotton, 1567, in the Trinity Chapel.

Monument to Lady Thornhurst, 1609 (St Michael's Chapel).

Archbishop of Canterbury, and a member of the old Plantagenet royal house. He died within a few hours of Mary herself, but despite a splendid funeral he was placed in a plain brick tomb with the simple inscription *Depositum Cardinalis Poli*, which lay neglected until its repair in the wake of the English Catholic revival in 1897.

Nearly opposite Pole, in the arcade of the Trinity Chapel, lies another cardinal, Odet de Coligny, Archbishop of Toulouse. Coligny was a renegade who espoused the cause of Huguenot Protestantism in sixteenth-century France (his brother was one of those massacred in the wholesale slaughter of the Huguenots in Paris on St Bartholomew's Day) and visited England on several occasions. Dying in 1571 he was supposed to have been poisoned by his valet, in the pay of the Catholic League. The coffin was temporarily encased in brick, awaiting its return to France, and thus it has remained. Huguenots, incidentally, have worshipped in the crypt of the Cathedral for four hundred years, since their expulsion from France at the time of the St Bartholomew massacre and again by Louis XIV at the close of the seventeenth century.

Monument to Sir John Boys, Recorder of Canterbury and steward to five successive archbishops (1612, north aisle of the nave).

Monument to the Hales family in the north aisle of the nave, c. 1596. Sir James Hales's death by drowning in the River Stour, is depicted in the painted panel, and the shipboard funeral of his son James during an expedition against the Spaniards in the carving above.

St Michael's Chapel (Warriors' Chapel), with the tomb of Margaret Holland (a descendant of Joan Holland, wife of the Black Prince) and her two husbands, 1437 (see text, p. 73).

Detail of Thomas Thornhurst and his wife, 1627 (St Michael's Chapel).

At the end of the ninteenth century, being fewer in number, they were given the Black Prince's chantry in which to hold their services, as they still do today.

The Cathedral has several richly decorated examples of Elizabethan and Jacobean monumental art, fascinating reflections of the taste of the period. Among these is the enjoyable narrative tomb of Sir James Hales and his son (see p. 71). The family was twice afflicted with disaster: the elder Sir James, a judge of Common Pleas, was so harrassed in a quarrel with the vindictive Bishop Gardiner of Winchester that in 1554 he drowned himself in the River Stour: his son James died at sea, leading an expedition against the Spaniards in 1589. The shipboard funeral is represented on the tomb.

On the opposite side of the church in St Michael's Chapel, surrounding the fine alabaster figures of Lady Margaret Holland (d. 1437) and her two husbands, the Earl of Somerset and the Duke of Clarence, are further colourful memorials of the age of Shakespeare, Bacon and Sir Walter Raleigh. Two of the most elegant, those to Thomas Thornhurst and William Prude respectively (note the latter's charming epitaph), show the armoured effigies kneeling under curtains held back by attendant soldiers. St. Michael's has come to be known as the Warriors' Chapel as it has associations with local service units - including the former Royal East Kent Regiment, The Buffs. It now also houses the Book of Rememberance of its successor regiments, The Queen's Regiment and The Princess of Wale's Royal Regiment (Queen's and Royal Hampshires). A page is turned at a short Service every weekday at 11am.

Kneeling children, each carrying his or her own skull, on the Thornhurst monument, 1627 (St Michael's Chapel).

Chapel of Our Lady Martyrdom (the Dean's Chapel): portrait of Dean Isaac Bargrave, painted on copper by Cornelius Jansen, 1643.

Tomb of Thomas Thornhurst, 1627 (St Michael's Chapel).

Chapel of Our Lady Martyrdom (the Deans' Chapel): tomb of Dean John Boys, 1625.

Chapel of Our Lady Martyrdom (the Deans' Chapel): detail of carving on the tomb of Dean Charles Fotherby, 1619.

In the north-west transept, in the exquisite setting of the Deans' Chapel, an assembly of outstanding early-Baroque tombs recalls the spirit of the metaphysical poets in the uneasy years before the Civil War. The cathedral had been poorly administered during Queen Elizabeth's reign - we read of 'rude boys playing and running about in ye tyme of divine service' and of officers needed to keep out dogs - and it required somebody with the vision and determination of William Laud, consecrated archbishop in 1633, to try and restore a little of the beauty of holiness to the church. Unfortunately he was unable to proceed without tactlessness and undue severity and antagonized many people who might otherwise have favoured his reforms.

The Dean during Laud's primacy was Isaac Bargrave, member of an old Kentish family, who had been chaplain to Nicholas Wotton's son, the great diplomatist and poet Sir Henry Wotton, during his embassy to Venice. Bargrave of course quarrelled with Laud, who called him peevish and petty, but when the Civil War arrived he took the Royalist side, exposing himself and his family to assault and outrage from the Parliamentarian soldiery. His memorial includes a portrait painted on copper by Cornelius Jansen (see p. 74). Wotton, incidentally, left Bargrave his

Memorial to Orlando Gibbons, 1626, by Nicholas Stone (nave, north aisle).

viola de gamba 'which hath been with me twice in Italy, in which country I first contracted with him an unremovable affection'.

Bargrave's predecessors John Boys and Charles Fotherby both have highly imaginative tombs. Boys, one of the best-read men of his day, is framed in an arch made of piled books, and the learned and pious Fotherby, a Lincolnshire man who had earlier been Archdeacon of Canterbury, has a tomb chest covered with carefully simulated human bones.

To the same period, of Anglicanism increasingly challenged by Puritan alternatives, belong the delicate marble bust of the composer Orlando Gibbons and the sumptuous Laudian font. Gibbons, an immensely versatile master, at home in vocal, instrumental and keyboard composition, died here in 1625 while awaiting the arrival from Dover of Charles I and Henrietta Maria, for whom, as a court composer, he may have been preparing celebratory music. The portrait bust, with its powerful contrast of white against black, was carved in the following year, for £35, by Nicholas Stone, the leading monumental artist of his day. As for the font, hidden from the Puritans and reassembled in 1660, it is a rare and remarkable survival of Caroline church furnishing, handsomely carved with the figures of the Evangelists and topped with a grandly tapering cover with its original pulley for lifting.

Font and font cover, presented in 1639 by Bishop Warner of Rochester (nave, west end).

Chapter 7 1660 to Modern Times

The Civil War brought widespread desecration to the fabric and furnishings of Canterbury Cathedral. Puritan irreverence was embodied in such wholesale outrages as those of Colonel Sandys's troopers, who shut the clergy out of the church while they overthrew the altar, tore down hangings. damaged the lectern, the organ and some of the monuments, and tore up bibles and prayer books. Later the medieval stained glass received similar attention when the egregious Richard Culmer, a worthy counterpart to his East Anglian contemporary Dowsing and described as 'a godly and orthodox divine', led the destruction of 'many window-images or pictures in glass . . . and many idolls of stone'. 'Rattling down proud Becket's glassy bones' was how Culmer himself described it.

At the restoration of the English monarchy in 1660, the Cathedral was in a wretched condition after years of neglect. Partly ruinous, with much of the timber and lead stripped from the roof, it had also been plundered of most of its moveable or detachable contents, as well as sustaining considerable losses to its archive and library. As much as possible was now reinstated, including the doors to the Christ Church gateway, a noble pair of carved wooden leaves bearing the arms of the cathedral and those of the see impaling the arms of Archbishop William Juxon, who had attended Charles I during his last moments on the scaffold at Whitehall in 1649.

Further evidence of the zeal with which the chapter undertook repairs is shown in the imposing set of return stalls across the western end of the choir (see p. 82). These, typical of the best woodwork of their period, are the work of the carver Roger Davis, who signed his design in the presence of the scientist and architect Robert Hooke in 1676 and completed the stalls six years later. Contemporary with these is the gawkily primitive painted panel of King Charles I as a martyred saint, now hanging in the north quire aisle and closely based on the frontispiece to the Royalist propaganda book *Eikon Basilike*, supposedly by the king himself, but probably by Dr Gauden, Bishop of Worcester. The post-Restoration cult of 'Charles the Martyr' produced at least two churches dedicated to the king, at Falmouth and Tunbridge Wells.

The tremendous late Baroque throne presented by Archbishop Tenison in 1704 fell a victim to Victorian concepts of good taste, which substituted the existing neo-Gothic piece now in the quire. The handsome early eighteenth-century monument to Admiral Sir George Rooke stands, in the Warriors' Chapel. His capture of Gibraltar in 1704 was to give England an invaluable Mediterranean foothold. The periwigged bust on its pedestal, and the marine relief sculpture below, are probably the work of Edward Stanton, a brilliant portraitist in marble.

The age to which these things belong was, when all is said and done, one of the most supine and apathetic in English church history. Typical of the contemporary spirit of Canterbury and its archbishops were the comments of Dr Herring, Archbishop from 1747 to 1757, on the

Carved oak panel on the Christ Church Gate, 1660-3.

Return stalls at west end of the choir, carved by Roger Davis, 1704.

King of Sardinia's request for relics of St Anselm. He would be glad, he said, to exchange 'the rotten remains of a rebel to his King, a slave to the Popedom, and an enemy to the married clergy, for ease and indulgence to one living Protestant'. He would 'make a conscience of palming on the simpletons any old bishop with the name of Anselm'. The canons residentiary matched this style perfectly. Dr Nelson, brother to the great admiral, 'a rough man, fitted to be a country squire', used to take *The Times* into prayers with him, seldom noticing the rustle of its pages as he was very deaf. As his brother's heir, he later became Canon the Duke of Bronte - a mixture of titles which must surely be rare. His brother's famous mistress Lady Hamilton, incidentally, once sang a solo in the cathedral after evensong, to the admiration of clergy otherwise scandalized by her notorious past.

With the revival of Anglican worship and commitment which took place during the early Victorian decades, notable changes came about at Canterbury. Though Canon Arthur Penryn Stanley, for example, continued the tradition of absenteeism among the residentiary canons, it was his masterly sketches of the Cathedral's past and of the men associated with it, in *Historical Memorials of Canterbury*, which drew attention to a crying need for restoration of the fabric of the Cathedral. A series of highly competent and enthusiastic deans, Alford, Payne-Smith and Farrar (famous also as the author of the school classic *Eric or Little by Little*) undertook

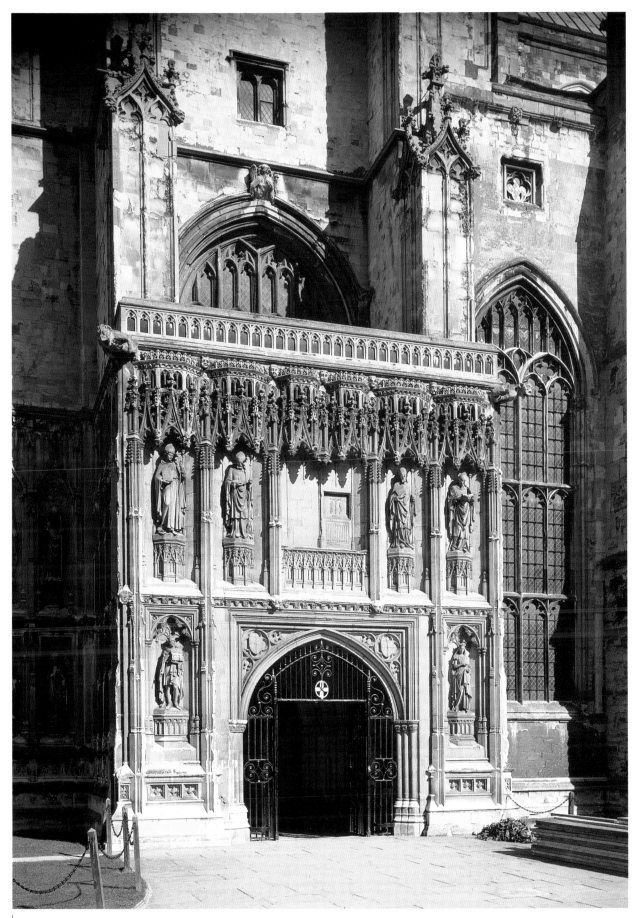

The south-west porch, restored with statues added by Theodore Pfyffers, 1862.

Monument to Admiral Sir George Rooke, attributed to Edward Stanton, 1708.

extensive repairs to the building. Despite occasionally thoughtless demolitions, Canterbury Cathedral suffered a good deal less than others in England from the heavy hands of high-minded refurbishers. To this period belong the north-west tower, the renewed south-west porch, with its statues by Theodore Pfyffers (1862), the oak stalls in the quire by Sir Gilbert Scott (1879) and the archbishop's throne by George Austin (1844).

At the close of the century, when Archbishop Frederick Temple acceded to the primacy, the Old Palace, on the corner of the Cathedral to the north west, was restored, incorporating as much of the earlier fabric as possible. The architect, W. D. Caroe, using what has been called 'a fidgety picturesque Tudor style', included a chapel and a lecture room, and the Archbishops of Canterbury were, for the first time in three centuries, able to live comfortably and adequately within the shadow of the mother church of their diocese. Temple was, in fact, the first Archbishop since Laud to live at Canterbury, just as his predecessor, Benson, had been the first Archbishop since Pole to be buried there: the primates of the intervening period had normally resided in the archiepiscopal palaces at Croydon or Addington. and had been buried at Addington leaving if anything only an empty cenotaph in the Cathedral itself. Indeed, this was altogether a period when the clergy associated with the Cathedral began gradually to show a greater appreciation of Canterbury's significance. From the Reformation until the middle of the ninteenth century, archbishops had almost always been enthroned by proxy, the dean or one of the Cathedral clergy taking the place of the primate, but in 1848 Archbishop Sumner

Clearing the Infirmary Arches: water-colour, artist unknown, c. 1868. The infirmary ruins, patched up in Tudor times to provide residential accommodation, had become uninhabitable by the mid-19th century and were cleared by Dean Alford.

revived the ancient custom of personal enthronement in the Cathedral. Though the *Church Times* in 1874 still remarked on the slovenliness of evensong ('when the procession straggled in, a more untidy and illfitting set of surplices could not have been seen, many of them not even having the recommendation of cleanliness'), the standard of devotion in the cathedral improved during the last decades of the Victorian age.

The Cathedral of today welcomes visitors from all over the world. Some 2 million come each year, and the Visits Department is responsible for their care. Within that the Education Department provides a whole range of activities and resources for all ages.

View of the south-west side of the Cathedral, with the twin west towers and the south-west porch.

St Augustine's Chair, traditionally used for the enthronement of archbishops. Dating from the 13th century, it certainly never had anything to do with St Augustine personally, and may have been made by Archbishop Stephen Langton at the time of the translation of Becket's remains. It could possibly be a copy of Augustine's original *cathedra* of the early 7th century.

The daily worship is the traditional round of Morning and Evening Prayer, with the Eucharist. With that are the great national and ecclesiastical occasions, as well as the devotions of pilgrim groups and individual people. Candles are lit and burn in various places in the building, representing prayers offered. Intercessions are left at the Prayer Desk in the Crypt to be included in the morning worship. Prayer cards are taken away as a token of people's responses to God's presence.

All of this is kept in place by a competent and dedicated administration, which sustains the constant flow of necessary resources upon which both the great fabric and its many activities depend.

Canterbury Cathedral stands as both a symbol of God's abiding glory and presence, and also a monument of men and women's continuing dedication and achievement.

The nave by candlelight, during a carol service.

 **The Dean & Chapter**

The Dean
The Canon Treasurer
The Senior Canon
The Canon Librarian
The Archdeacon of Canterbury

Total Staff   **549**

Works Department

Carpenters	3
Cathedral Wardens	12
Electricians	2
Gardeners	8
Labourers	6
Stonemasons	20
Painters	1
Plumbers	1
Scaffolders	2
Security Office	1
Stained Glass Conservators	8

Worship

Clergy (The Precentor)	6
Organists	2
Lay Clerks	12
Choristers	18
Virgers	8
Cleaners	8
'Holy Dusters'	30

Administration

Heads of Department	13
Accounts	6
Archives	12
Friends' Office	3
Library	4
Porter	1
Secretaries	8
Receptionists	2

Visits

Education Department	5
Gift Shop	35
Guides, Assistants and Chaplains	250
Visits Department	3
Welcome Centre	
Shepherds	20
Welcomers	34

The Cathedral from the War Memorial Gardens was once the chapter bowling green and originally the convent gardens.

Both paid staff and volunteers day by day serve the needs of the Cathedral. There are seasonal fluctuations in actual numbers involved. The list opposite represents the typical complement.

The Cathedral from the south.

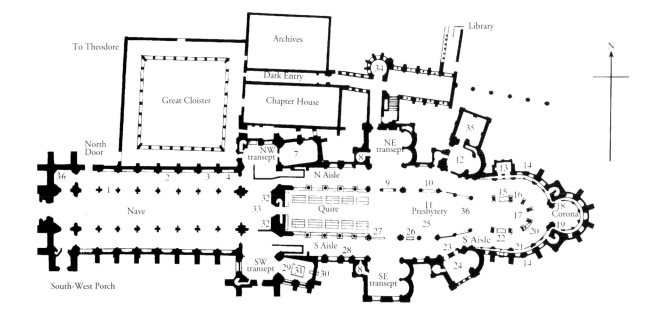

Cathedral

1 Font
2 Memorial to Orlando Gibbons
3 Memorial to Sir John Boys
4 The Hales Monument
5 Tomb of Archbishop Peckham
6 The Martyrdom
7 The Chapel of Our Lady Martyrdom (The Dean's Chapel)
8 Anselm's towers
9 Tomb of Archbishop Chichele
10 Tomb of Archbishop Bourchier
11 Site of the shrine of St Alphege
12 St Andrew's Chapel
13 Henry IV's chantry (Chapel of St Edward the Confessor)
14 The Miracle windows
15 Tomb of Henry IV and Joan of Navarre
16 Tomb of Dean Wotton
17 Site of Thomas Becket's shrine from 1220 to 1538
18 Tomb of Cardinal Pole
19 Tomb of Archbishop Frederick Temple

20 Tomb of Cardinal Odet de Coligny
21 Tomb of Archbishop Hubert Walter
22 Tomb of the Black Prince
23 Tomb of Archbishop Meopham
24 St Anselm's Chapel
25 Site of the shrine of St Dunstan
26 Tomb of Archbishop Stratford
27 Archbishop's throne
28 Tomb of Prior Henry of Eastry
29 St Michael's Chapel (The Warriors' Chapel)
30 Tomb of Archbishop Stephen Langton
31 Tomb of Lady Margaret Holland, the Earl of Somerset and the Duke of Clarence
32 The pulpitum (quire screen)
33 Base of the Bell Harry tower
34 Water tower
35 Treasury/Vestiarium
36 St Augustine's Chair

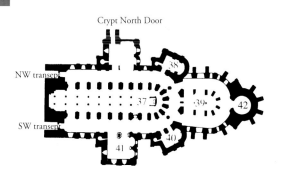

Crypt

37 Chapel of Our Lady Undercroft
38 Chapel of the Holy Innocents
39 Site of Thomas Becket's tomb from 1170 to 1220
40 St Gabriel's Chapel
41 The Black Prince's chantry (now the Huguenots' chapel)
42 Jesus Chapel

The Nave, completed in 1405

Cathedral Information

Service Times

Sundays:	*Holy Communion*	1800
	Matins said (or sung by the King's School)	0930
	*Sung Eucharist**	1100
	Evensong (sung)	1515
	*Evening Service**	1830
	*with Sermon	
Weekdays:	*Matins* (said)	0730
	Holy Communion	0800
	Wednesdays	also at 1100
	Thursdays	also at 1815
	Major Saints Days (sung)	1015
	Evensong (sung)	1730
Saturdays:	*Matins*	0930
	Choral Evensong	1515

Opening Times

0900–1900 (Summer) / 0900–1700 (Winter)
1230–1430 and 1630–1730 Sunday
Access is limited at the times of services
N.B. The Cathedral or parts of it may have to be closed from time to time for special circumstances, without prior notice.

Guided Tours**

Arrangements for advance bookings by groups and organizations can be made. Foreign language tours can be arranged. Special tours of an extended character and longer duration may be arranged in advance throughout the year.

General guided tours, lasting one hour, take place at regular intervals throughout the day. **Audio-visual presentations** run regularly in several languages. **Audio tours** in seven languages are available most days, starting from the west end of the Nave.

Details can be obtained from the Visits Office, 11 The Precincts, Canterbury, Kent CT1 2EH
Tel: (01227) 762862, Fax: (01227) 865222
Email: visits@canterbury-cathedral.org, Website: www.canterbury-cathedral.org
** Only accredited Cathedral guides are permitted to operate inside the Cathedral.

The Cathedral Shop

Canterbury Cathedral Shop, 25 Burgate, Canterbury, Kent CT1 2HA
Tel: (01227) 865300, Fax: (01227) 865333, Email: enquiries@cathedral-enterprises.co.uk
0930–1730 Monday–Saturday
1030–1630 Sunday
A mail order service is available. Please call us for a brochure or contact
mailorder@cathedral-enterprises.co.uk
www.cathedral-enterprises.co.uk

The Georgian first-floor gallery features books, arts and crafts amongst a selection of interesting replicas and other items.

All profits go to the upkeep of the Cathedral.